Birding Peru 2015

An account of a birdwatching trip to Peru in
October 2015, with observations about the
country, its people and fellow travellers. Plus a
coda of Tenerife in 2013 and Madrid in 2004.

Also by Andy Gibb

Fiction:
Clearing the Brushes
Tales Told by an Idiot
Let the Time Come

Birding:
The British Birding Year
The Honeyeaters' Tree
California Wakin' 2000-3

BIRDING PERU 2015

Andy Gibb

First published 2017

Second edition © 2025 Andy Gibb

ISBN: 978-1-326-67768-8

http://www.lulu.com/spotlight/birdtours

To the staff at Monte Horeb, Cusco

Table of Contents

The Plan

Boasting a possible 1,922 bird species, Peru has to rank as one of the top countries on the planet. Among these are such charismatic species as Andean condor, cock-of-the-rock, toucans, macaws, the hoatzin, trogons, jacamars and tanagers. The last three families come in all the colours and combinations of the rainbow. Everyone loves hummingbirds and the Peruvian roster includes specimens with outrageous tails and the largest hummer in the world. For the birder, more subtle families like tinamous, ovenbirds, currasows, guans, antbirds and a whole raft of flycatchers are mainly endemic to South America and thus an equal draw.

In three weeks I could only expect to see a small fraction of the avifauna, the more so because I was unfamiliar with most of the families: their identification would be a challenge. Scratching the surface was inevitable, especially if sampling several habitats. These are pretty much predetermined to be the coast, where you have to land from Europe, the mountains and the jungle.

Machu Picchu, and hence Cusco, is a no-brainer for one's first time in the Andes, so that leaves a choice for descending to the jungle. Pantiacolla was my solution with a two-day bus ride down to their lodge in Amazonia and the same back up. A couple of overnight stops on the way would provide birds at different elevations.

While booking the itinerary, my Helm field guide, *Birds of Peru*, arrived, appropriately from Amazon. It took weeks to scour through it to construct a list of easy, harder, challenging and downright difficult species on each stage of the journey. A bizarre find at Portland Bird Observatory was *Where To Watch Birds in Peru* by Thomas Valqui, which helped the process. I also downloaded pictures from the Web to my phone. All this preparation stood me in good stead as a fair number of birds were a cinch to identify.

Nearly as important as the destination was the small matter of which route to fly to Lima. No airline flew direct from Britain, so a stopover was inevitable.

Madrid

It had to be there or Amsterdam and the Spanish capital had birding form (see the appendix for an account of hawfinches, spotless starlings, Casa de Campo and El Pardo). This time I elected for a hotel near the airport on the grounds that it was a short taxi hop after a late flight.

Big logistical flaw. Cabs away from Barajas carry a surcharge of 30 euros.

30 euros. That's over £20.

Savour that amount and wonder why anyone falls for it twice. Sufficient mugs must pass through just the once to make the scam worthwhile.

To rub salt, my driver had no clue where my hotel was and dumped me outside a block of serviced apartments. Only after wandering up and down a bleak street did I find the Axor Feria and my bed for the remainder of the night.

OK, I'll dwell no further on Madrileño taxis.

What about the birds this time? Spotless starlings remained obvious, from my window the next morning, and venturing into the hotel forecourt brought me a wholly unexpected pied flycatcher. I had to double-check it but needn't have bothered because the whole city was dripping with them. They were the avian highlight of the weekend and, by the way, unrelated to South American flycatchers.

The rest of Saturday was given over to social affairs as my lady friends, Justine and Sylvia, and my brother – all down from Edinburgh – had contrived to stay in town. This meant finding a metro station to join them.

El Capricho was the closest to the Axor but it took some getting to as motorways carve up that north-west corner of Madrid and make walking near impossible. Hence the need for a taxi from the airport—oops, sorry, I promised I wouldn't mention that again! Anyway, all my party managed to coordinate by the evening to meet at a bar right by Plaza de España station, where euros magically transformed into beers, gin and tapas. Then I had to return to my remote quarter but a couple of decent bars on the way eased the journey.

For the Sunday £3.81 on Expedia had secured me a nearby hire car but this time the pedestrian hostility of the neighbourhood defeated me. My search for the rental compound took me deeper and deeper into an industrial wasteland complete with barking dogs and I don't cope with either. Discretion seemed in order and I spent the rest of the day dodging light showers at Parque El Capricho and Juan Carlos I, which I'd worked a decade previously.

It didn't disappoint this time with tree sparrows, a serin, Iberian green woodpecker, Sardinian warbler and the year's sole spotted flycatcher. These were all birds I'd seen before, so there were no lifers at this point for my world list.

Lima

On Monday the hotel shuttle – ha! sod you, taxi drivers – took me to Madrid's Terminal 4 and a wee train under the runway on to 4S, where the S stands for satellite – yes, even in Spanish.

A 12-hour Iberia flight landed me at Lima more or less on time. Having given up my window seat to a couple who wanted to sit together, I had nothing more to view than the seat-back entertainment... oh, and the tailcam on take-off and landing; that was new to me and pretty neat. In my aisle seat the toilet was easy to access but where was the beer to fuel these visits? One measly quarter-litre can was all that arrived.

This kept me awake to take in three movies. The first was a repeat of *L.A. Confidential* – one of my top ever films. Then *San Andreas* – more for the effects than anything else but turbulence at the appropriate moments made the earthquakes quite thrilling; despite being Hollywood hokum, the film was bearable. Finally, the more recent *Spy* was a hoot and doubtless funnier without Iberia's censorship for language.

We hit South America at Georgetown and presumably spent the next three hours passing over the Amazon Basin and the view would largely have been of trees. To add insult to injury the window-seat people had pulled down their blinds, so who knows what was passing underneath – cattle ranches, gold mines, oil refineries, palm plantations?

My first glimpse of the continent was of a super-dry landscape on the descent to Lima, and rows of cargo ships at anchor outside Callao, the city's port.

The landing itself was on a par. I'd done too many of these myself but a fair few passengers broke into applause. That used to happen twenty years ago in the infancy of transatlantic aviation and it was kind of cheesy to hear the tradition living on. Perhaps solely on Latin flights. My clapping is reserved for the second attempt. Yup, this has happened.

Negotiating baggage reclaim was a cinch and the customs lady was welcoming and cheerful. I warmed to Peru immediately. The hour or so for all this meant night had fallen by the time I found my taxi.

Prebooking it was a Good Idea: the ride to Hostal el Patio in Miraflores took an hour in manic traffic and it was reassuring to have confidence in my driver. Other cabbies touting for business could have been anyone and I certainly couldn't imagine catching a collectivo, which is a totally anarchic sort of bus. Most of those vehicles were so beaten up their owners couldn't have cared about a scrape or two. My taxi was relatively modern but all the same it nosed into the most impossible gaps, disregarded lane markings and beeped its mandatory horn to bore our way to the hotel. One popular tactic was tootling along in the outside lane, before veering across the others to turn right; this was perfectly acceptable. It was so South American and made Madrid look sedate.

A massive police presence couldn't ameliorate all the confusion. Indeed, their bikes weaving in and out with lights flashing, and officers blowing whistles on point duty merely served to heighten it.

"World Bank," growled my driver.

Of course. I had been aware that the International Monetary Fund and their cronies in crime were having one of their beanos in Lima. Now I began to see gaggles of cops on street corners and outside banks. Was the rest of Peru thus devoid of law and order?

By Miraflores the police had multiplied to all the hotels, and guns were much in evidence, although Hostal el Patio didn't rate a guard. It must have been too downmarket for the money-swilling minions of capitalism.

But it was lovely. Don't be fooled by the name: it was a hotel but not a swanky one. It also boasted a charming verdant courtyard, complete with elegant fountain. My room was rustic but comfortable and came with table and chairs outside on the communal veranda.

Thanks to the six-hour time difference it didn't take much to wake me at sunrise, i.e. well before six. As it happened, the *toodle-ooh* of west Peruvian doves pulled me out of bed and became my first lifer of the trip. These are the size and build of our collared doves with a prominent white wing patch; they are the dove of the coastal strip and they started a 20-lifer day, which is OK for a mega-city but bad for a birding trip. I was caught between the tourist and twitching stools. Contrary to expectations though, I identified every species.

Not far from the hotel a raucous, explosive series of calls alerted me to another lifer – scrub blackbirds flitting between urban trees. My pre-trip preparation had covered all the day's birds but I scribbled notes and rough sketches all the same. Lugging a field guide the size of Peru's was right out of the question and in any case burying one's nose in a book is a guarantee of missing much action. The same goes for electronic aids. Field notes are the one essential for those unexpected or cryptic species. The sole technology that distinguished me from Mr Darwin, the

Reverend White et al were my ever-present binoculars.

Without so much as following a map, I found Parque 7 de Junio with Parque Kennedy, the one green space in Miraflores, and house wrens followed on to the year list. At the time that was a widespread bird, all the way up to the USA, where I'd lived in 1997/8 and 2000-2. Only last year the IOU split the species along a line through southern Mexico. So this sighting has become what we birders call an armchair tick.

A long-tailed mockingbird soon heralded a flood of the rest of the life birds; southern beardless tyrannulet, amazilia hummingbird, Harris hawk, bananaquit – in its own odd family between orioles and buntings – and saffron finch were among them. All this despite the attentions of most of the feral cats in Lima. Seriously, the park sprouted cats and the locals fed them and petted them; maybe that's the way it works with nine million inhabitants crammed into the metropolis.

My favourite birds of the day had to be the punky tyrannulets: these tiny South American flycatchers were ubiquitous and double cute with their crests and neat little bills. The mockingbirds were as bold as their north American cousins and came a close second. Vermilion flycatchers were up there as a welcome reprise of three sightings during the early 2000s in California.

Now I have to talk toilets. What could be odd about toilets? But the etiquette is different in Peru. I didn't learn this until many days into the trip and had been happily flushing paper down the loo, when paper was needed if you get my drift. This buggers up their sewage systems, so the routine is to wrap the tissue up and dispose of it in a bin.

Gross, or what? Gross but necessary. And apparently I've been oblivious to this routine elsewhere in the world, including Europe.

On my second foray into the city, after breakfast and ablutions, the first rufous-collared sparrow made its entrance; along with the wren it was pretty ubiquitous – so too feral pigeon of course. My route this Lima morning took me down to brown cliffs where black vultures were soon obvious. The colour of these cliffs lent them a fragile appearance and nets draped over them reinforced the impression. One earthquake and the whole lot would crumble.

Roads snaked up from the sea in natural gullies to Miraflores and this all reminded me of Bournemouth with its chines. All it needed was a few funiculars, fish'n'chips and a pier. Oh, and wetter weather.

Lima is in a desert. A paltry 0.3 inches of rain sprinkle it per year. Being on the coast however, neotropic cormorant, Belcher's gull, Peruvian pelican, Inca tern and Peruvian booby went onto the life list. Yes, yes, I know: booby – ha-ha. Good thing Peru doesn't have shags. Nor tits. Right, that's some of the puerile jokes out of the way.

Perched on top of these friable cliffs was the new posh shopping and dining centre of Larco Mar and to welcome visitors, an old friend of mine. Paddington Bear, complete with Union Jack duffel-coat. I'm sure that wasn't in the books. I'm equally sure that his childhood influence was behind my idea to visit Peru. I say this because my 2008/9 visit to Australia grew from similar roots – pictures of kangaroos and an aborigine on my bedroom wall as I was growing up. These currents run deep.

A party of Dutch and American birders was working the cliffs. "It's the end of our holiday," they explained, "and our wives are in the mall, so we're taking a final opportunity..."

"Falcon!" one of them called and a smart little American kestrel patrolled by – my first for over six years.

Hard on its heels was the trip's first of the tanager family, which has to be even more colourfully diverse than parrots. Bright yellow western tanagers had been reliable migrants to California, and the rest of the USA had produced one apiece of the brilliant red summer and scarlet tanagers. These are rare species in Peru and the bird at Miraflores' cliffs was the widespread blue-grey tanager. It's muted in comparison, the blue in its wings being a notch more turquoise than the grey of the rest of its plumage. In addition the population in Lima is introduced but I would see plenty of wild birds in the interior; the Amazonian subspecies had white shoulders to add to its distinction.

The usual birding doldrums kicked in early afternoon, so it was the perfect time to eat. To my shame my first Peruvian dinner was a pizza at Mamma Lola: I wasn't ready for ceviche, which is basically raw seafood but marinated in lemon juice and chilis. It sounds delicious but I needed to be sure that the restaurant serving it wasn't going to poison me so early in the trip.

However, I was ready for Cusqueña, a drink that had eluded me thus far. It was easily the best Peruvian beer since the local Pilsen was a tad watery. Yet, all the brews contributed at the end of the accounting trail to the profits of SABMiller – same as Foster's and Grolsch. What's worse was that every bottle of water was labelled Coca-Cola and guess who put the stuff in the bottles?

If you said SABMiller, have a hatload of cynicism points.

The meal wasn't the end of the day for me despite being 10pm in Europe. The six-hour time difference left an hour's daylight until the swift tropical dusk fell. My evening restarted at Mamma Lola with a pisco sour, which is the local brandy with lime juice, syrup, egg white, and Angostura bitters over ice – yum-yum. But one (large) was enough plus a couple more beers at the Old Pub to send me to bed.

Wednesday, and you remember the 0.3 inches of rain a year? I swear more than that was falling as I woke up. I have this effect: in 2008 the otherwise bone-dry South Australia had drizzled in the same way before it set in to solid rain and then a deluge. The Lima episode remained gentle but rendered the exposed floors and tiled walkways of Hostal el Patio treacherous.

I made it to breakfast unscathed, and after ablutions braved the drizzle to find Bosque El Olivar, on the road into the central business district. This translates to olive woodland and it may once have been that before Lima swallowed it up.

On the way there I passed a most curious display from one bird: it flew up and back straight down to the same perch with a sort of grasshopper song. This was quite the puzzle until later views of an obvious blue-black grassquit repeating the performance solved it.

At least one, and probably three, peregrine falcons enlivened the walk. I wasn't expecting them since my field guide had their status as rare but they were unmistakable and a caution that the book wasn't infallible. Published by Helm, it is however indispensable and the work of years, so respect to those involved.

El Olivar turned out to be tiny when I arrived, except I wasn't there. By walking a sort of spiral I happened upon the over-manicured park, which was the correct destination. Thanks to the heavy hands of the keepers, it was devoid of anything bar more vermilion flycatchers and my sole house sparrows of the trip.

Determined not to return by the main road, I eventually wound down by Huaca Pucllana. This is a bulky pre-Incan earthwork like a boil in the fabric of Lima. But croaking ground doves and white-winged parakeets on the way made it worthwhile.

Despite a hefty cloud cover during this morning, my face was beginning to feel decidedly raw. So close to the equator, the sun's rays penetrate and if I hadn't donned a baseball cap, I dread to imagine what state my skin would have been in. As it was, I had to seek out SPF 50 lotion later in the day for fear of crisping to a poppadom.

My route returned me to the Miraflores coast, where serrated ranks of thousands of seabirds patrolled the inshore waters. Cormorants, boobies, pelicans, gulls and terns could have hidden rarities but the seething mass made individuals impossible to distinguish. There must have been some upwelling of marine life, maybe connected with the ever strengthening El Niño, to attract such numbers of predators.

More amazing than this weight of birds was the sheer obliviousness of strollers along the cliffs. How disconnected we are to the real currents of the world. If it doesn't show on our iPhones, it doesn't exist.

The final species of the day was a pair of blackish oystercatchers down at the water's edge. I'd had to descend one of the "chines" to get there, the principal attraction being a colony of Inca terns that carpeted the roof of a nearby pier. These birds were so habituated to humans that they'd pose mere feet away and how splendid they were in their black plumage with white curling whiskers.

Climbing back up the cliffs brought home to me how exhausted I was, probably from the sun, and I collapsed on to my bed for the rest of the afternoon. So the last birds I saw in Lima were a couple of scrub blackbirds, attracted to our courtyard fountain in the dying light of the day.

Cusco

A second mad taxi drive got me safely onto my eye-opening flight out to Cusco. The ascent from Lima revealed a panoply of high-rise dwellings stretching away from the coast; Miraflores was a tiny moneyed enclave. Then the desert took over. Ridge upon ridge of dessicated land groped towards the sea as we climbed and began to attain the snow-clad peaks of the Andes.

It's always been my joke that I should visit the mountains named after me; now here they were and they were serious. Just one small town clung to their flanks on the entire route to Cusco; the Rockies had been hospitable by comparison. The winds funnelled by the mountains rose and shoved our plane around on the one path to the airport as peaks closed in on us. We were so tiny.

But like an indestructible insect we touched down and the comforts of civilisation took over to whisk us through the airport. This time there was no pre-booked taxi to shepherd me to safety, so one of the circling sharks drove me to Hospedaje Monte Horeb for 25 soles. That's a touch over five quid but 25 sounds much more damaging. There was getting to be little that *ad hoc* taxi drivers could do right for me.

Monte Horeb was more basic than el Patio and was set on the first floor around an inner courtyard. This arrangement was commonplace in Cusco and until one sussed that businesses were set back in them, it was difficult to find some places. My driver managed to navigate me to the right location and most of the afternoon remained at my disposal basically to chill out.

Aware that the altitude of over 11,000 feet could be a crippler, I took a slow, slow stroll round the local squares. A light-headed sensation and a little out of breath were the worst of my symptoms.

The centre of Cusco is compact with narrow streets connecting the plazas. Traffic was less manic than Lima's but still didn't observe the niceties of road discipline. Cops at many intersections helped pedestrians with an even chance of crossing the road. Or the sheer weight of tourists walking the town overwhelmed the vehicles. Native Peruvians were less numerous outside as they ran the shops and otherwise hawked their wares wherever they could.

One of these "wares" was *massaje* – young ladies offering me *massaje*. Was that what it means back home? I have no idea but it's one to research!

Most obvious of the few city centre birds were Chiguanco thrushes, easy to recognise by being a dead ringer for our blackbird. My old friends, the rufous-collared sparrows, continued to make themselves known but one similar-sized bird flitting into a bush by Plaza San Francisco was a puzzler. All it displayed was a hood with an olive green back and hints of rufous but not at all in the sparrows' configuration. The following day more sightings of the same species allowed me to recognise it for Peruvian sierra finch.

Perched above the cathedral and less problematic was a giant hummingbird. That was my the description of the individual and the name of the species. It is big moreover – the size of a small thrush – and able to hover nonetheless. So Thursday ended well with one of my target species.

Then I slept, which is a much touted way to pass through altitude adjustment, and next morning I felt up to tackling the slight climb away from the cathedral. My ultimate goal was Sacsayhuaman – its ruins, that's to say – not for any archaeological interest but its scrubby hillsides had potential for non-city birds. Translations of the name run all the way from Satisfied Falcon through Variable Hawk to the prosaic House of the Sun. I prefer the birdy versions.

These lanes were narrow cobbled roadways with even narrower pavements, stepped at the steepest inclines. It all put me in mind of the Roman streets at Herculaneum; they really were the oldest part of town. Not far up the hill a bridge crossed a small stream before diving under the city; like Bristol, Cusco was full of subterranean water.

This pathetic little trickle supported vegetation and, apart from harbouring a sierra finch to confirm my previous day's suspicion, it added hooded siskin and golden-billed saltator to the life list. The saltator is a member of the grosbeak family; in other words it's a finch with a very big bill, not surprisingly yellow in its case, and thus easy to identify.

I kept going up and made it the half mile or so to the entrance to Sexy Woman – that's how the name sounded to me. The entrance fee was as steep as the climb so I mentally scratched it from my bucket list and worked a nearby patch of scrub.

Midday, and hence the doldrums, was approaching. Birds were growing scarce, so all I managed was a ground dove, bare-faced as later consultation with the field guide suggested. In contrast to Spanish towns nothing flew above the rooftops, not a swallow, swift nor raptor (bar Sacsayhuaman) so it seemed I'd exhausted the day.

Three lifers when expectations were low wasn't all bad. Worse was to come after lunch, which I ate at a restaurant in one of the courtyards next to my hotel. This fare was billed as mountain cuisine, which is to say potatoes and rice with some sort of meat (chicken?) but the first course was interesting, being yucca.

Who'd have thought that? My family had a yucca in our Winchester front garden for years and never considered its edible properties; it wasn't dissimilar to parsnip and jolly pleasant. A glass of chicha accompanied the meal, and another. It's a corn beer and I figured I was altitude-ready for alcohol by then.

The bad news in the afternoon was that I'd lost my jungle trip with Pantiacolla: too few punters had subscribed to make it worth their while. Expecting that in the absence of recent communication from them, I dropped in to confirm the worst and so was left with a day or two to mull over filling the missing week.

The Cusco birding improved on Saturday. I checked out another stream that mainly flowed underground but this one, Rio Saphi, as it tumbled down a gorge, intimated that waterbirds were possible. My first species though was aerial as a large raptor cruised one of the defile's ridges. The bird's short triangular tail made it all black-chested buzzard-eagle and my life list was back on the move.

As it was, the Saphi was trickling, not tumbling, and my efforts to conjure something out of its watery void came to nought. Upon looking up, the retreating shapes of a dozen large dark birds flapped their broad wings upstream. They disappeared over one ridge and that was all I had. I cursed but even so their whole demeanour suggested ibis and puna ibis was indeed the only candidate.

Rather than return direct to town, I plodded up the flank of Sacsayhuaman. My reward was five more lifers, including the sole spinetail I saw on the entire trip. It was my first ovenbird, a 300-strong family restricted to South America and one of the targets for the trip. The family's name derives from the material for some of the species' nests, which they build from clay.

My early start meant I was back downtown in plenty of time for lunch, so it was the perfect moment to sample ceviche. The Qosqo (note the different spelling) Beer House offered a fine trout-based sample. Trout is dead popular along the river valleys in this area and to my mind a safe option to eat raw. Of course a complementary Cusqueña was necessary.

My mistake here was eating out on the terrace. This meant a persistent succession of women trying to sell me crap. I don't begrudge them earning a crust, but not while I'm dining. I'd happily pay a surcharge to be left alone.

The final lifer of the day, and of Cusco itself, made its expected appearance. I've noted the absence of flying among the rooftops but post-lunch a handful of white-collared swifts did precisely that. Even without my binoculars they were easy to call.

It was time to consider my lost jungle trip and the afternoon became frantic as I wondered whether I could bear more time in the Andes. I could hire a car and drive up to lakes and high passes for their species. Or should I make my yellow fever jab pay and descend to the Amazon whatever?

Doing so by Expedia was out of the question: the flight alone would cost me £230. Old technology came to my rescue: a last-minute scour round the local bucket-shops netted me a ticket to Puerto Maldonado for under a hundred quid and an outfit called EcoAmazonia came up with accommodation at a little over £300 for five days. Their lodge was upstream from PM on the Madre de Dios and near the Bolivian border.

Somehow, compared with spending four days

bouncing along mountain roads on a bus, this was an improvement over the original plan.

Machu Picchu

So the train journey to these fabled ruins dawned and an early taxi ride to the outskirts of Cusco took me up past a few miles of its less salubrious suburbs. The ramshackle buildings, pot-holed road and feral dogs nosing piles of rubbish were evidence that not all was well with Peru. The rail company didn't move its terminus from San Pedro in the city centre to the remoteness of Poroy in the hope of educating tourists to this reality. No, it was probably more to do with the time and economics of slogging a train up the switchbacks out of Cusco. The more cynical might say it kept the local cabbies in business.

The route away from Poroy station reinforced the third-world impression as we passed animals plough-ing dusty fields under the guidance of frail peasants. The first settlement down the line, Anta, was shabby, at best.

We'd now passed obvious cattle egrets and a large heron that back home would have been a grey heron but the one candidate in my *Field Guide to the Birds of Machu Picchu and the Cusco Region* was Cocoi heron. Described as rare, it was thus unlikely but this was my first inkling that the book wasn't accurate. (I later counted the sighting as kosher). I'm reluctant to diss the guide because I'd met the author, Barry Walker, at the British BirdFair and had him sign my copy. He's also the honorary consul in Cusco – not bad for a lad from Stalybridge – but... inaccuracies are inaccuracies.

The most glaring of these had me believing that the dark birds hawking every river edge later in the train ride, and in Aguas Calientes, were torrent tyrannu-lets: that was how they looked in the drawings. I should have known they were black phoebes, having seen thousands in North America.

My seat-mate was from London. "I'm only here for a couple of days," he said. "I couldn't even explore Lima: my hotel was right by the airport and the cabbie said not to venture out at night there. It seemed like a good idea when I booked it."

He was right all the same: vast tracts of Lima were no-go areas for gringos.

Past Anta the line plunged between dry towering cliffs and became its touted scenic wonder. Into the Urubamba Valley at Ollantaytambo, torrent ducks and Andean gulls became common. The male ducks – yes, that's drakes to the pedants – had striking rusty underparts while the actual ducks sported black stripes on white heads. They made quite the dashing couples in the foaming, rocky midstream currents. They're not called torrent ducks for no reason.

I gawped my way to Aguas Calientes, which is the original name for the pueblo that found itself gateway and sole layover for the ruins of Machu Picchu. It is called Machu Picchu Pueblo now but we'll have none of that. The Urubamba meanwhile had lost all its liveliness thanks to a hydro-electric scheme that ran right under Machu Picchu.

The river's low level rendered waterbirds scarce but after settling in to my digs a wee afternoon jaunt along one bank did add green-and-white humming-bird to the life list. This is a hummingbird that's green and white; they must have been running out of names for such an abundant family. A tiny pale grey bird darted after insects by the water's edge but I could not identify it. Once back in Cusco my Helm field guide pointed me to the real torrent tyrannulet.

The old go-to of pizza was next in a restaurant overlooking the river and with the odd train rumbling past the front door. There are no cars in Aguas Calientes and no roads to reach it, so the railway did the job of Main Street. However, turning in early for a dawn start to the citadel next morning was an exercise in futility thanks to the town centre noise. You'd hope somewhere traffic-free in the middle of the Andes would be quiet overnight.

The world and his *mujer* were up at daybreak all the same and the queue for the bus to the ruins already snaked halfway through town. It was possible that walking instead would be quicker but the heat was climbing and I had no idea how far the hike would be. Very far and very steep, it turned out, so my decision to buy the one-way ticket – at the best part of ten quid, mind – was sound.

All the same, it took an hour until I reached the head of the queue. We shuffled down to the bus stop in fits and starts and the local hawkers sold "waterproof" ponchos to those in line, although tourists could have picked them up from the shops we passed. Local guides were much in evidence as they flitted in and out to the gringos in their care; they clearly knew how long the wait would be.

My bus descended a couple of hundred metres to cross the Urubamba before negotiating the switchbacks up to Machu Picchu.

Upon arrival coffee was definitely the first item on the agenda. A neat little open-air cafe, up from the main restaurant, provided a superb cup. Its terrace was on a level with treetops for a perfect view of arboreal species. Of course the ever-present rufous-collared sparrows hopped around and an American kestrel drifted past. The one new species was a Sierran elaenia, which is another South American flycatcher related to the tyrannulets. Most of this family is a combination of drab grey colours, yellow hints, wing bars and crests if you're lucky enough to see them. Figuring out the actual species is a question of instantly registering the combination you're seeing and not confusing it with any other. In short, tons of practice is needed.

The paths round the ruins were a bit of a cattle market, complete with one-way system, which was difficult to walk against so I went with the flow. Many visitors looked like they'd never walked farther than their own backyards and were making heavy weather of the many steps and narrow ledges. I learned later that the helicopter had been up in the afternoon to take one fatality off the mountain – not an unusual occurrence, I bet.

The crowd was by and large American, which accounts for the citadel's massive popularity. We're spoiled in Europe with ruins just as extensive but many times more ancient. The backdrop of clouded towering peaks and deep verdant valleys does mark Machu Picchu as special all the same.

Birds were never numerous but round the main site I did add white-tipped swift and Andean guan. A large ungainly grouse-like bird, the guan is not top of an average tourist's bucket list but it's in a strictly Latin American family. So for me it was a big first. I wasn't expecting it to be atop a bush and would have missed it had its perch not been on a terrace below me. This put the bird right at my eye-level. Even its small red wattle was visible.

For more productive habitat, I headed for the Sun Gate but the morning was wearing on and the doldrums were already kicking in. However, you remember the endemic flycatchers that are more a birder's delight? Well, a probable white-crested elaenia was on the route and a tufted tit-tyrant, which was the easier to identify by being massively streaky and sporting extravagant head feathers. A definite spectacled whitestart also appeared.

Its other name is redstart, which is a mite confusing. Our own redstart is called thus for its rusty undertail feathers. So far so good because the whitestart has white undertail feathers. As do countless birds, so it's not really a distinguishing feature. But why call a species red when it's actually white?

If that last paragraph lost you, you're not alone. And the name hardly does justice to the bird, which does appear to be wearing spectacles with its big yellow eyering and lores. It also has slaty grey wings and back, bright yellow underparts and the male tops it all off with a fiery red crown. This is one stunner.

Aware that my one-way bus ticket meant a long, hot tramp back down to Aguas Calientes, I didn't commit myself to the whole distance up to the Sun Gate and turned back. Pausing for more caffeine, I worked my way down the steps to the Urubamba.

It was tough on the knees but immediately worth it with a blue-necked tanager. Why the name concentrates on the neck is a mystery: the bird's entire head is a cobalt blue contrasting with a body so dark blue that it looks black. There's more: yellow wing flashes and rump qualify the species as one of the more colourful tanagers, and that's saying something.

The second noteworthy bird was a simple exercise in browns and whites but no less exciting for that. Like the tanager, it forages in the canopy. That's to say at the tops of trees, which is why trekking down a steep incline works: one is thus on a level with the canopy on the lower slopes. So, a streaked xenops came into view and was immediately recognisable by being brown and streaky with obvious white facial stripes. The species was my second ever ovenbird and priceless as such.

Back to the white/redstarts. My next species was a slate-throated whitestart, its distinction from spectacled whitestart being a lack of yellow round the face and throat. Otherwise, the bird followed the same stunning colour scheme. I was beginning to wonder if I'd dropped ayahuasca the night before.

(Ayahuasca is a ceremonial medicine – sic – in Amazonia, i.e. their equivalent of our magic mushrooms. Certain tour companies offer it as part of the native experience.)

These three birds had appeared in quick succession before the descent to the river turned into a slog – a sweaty hour-long slog – and I hoped my insect repellent wasn't sluicing off. The forest below Machu Picchu had stung many a birder who hadn't applied the stuff.

Finally down by the Urubamba a bigger rusty bird was a puzzler and subsequent investigation has led me to 90% certainty of cliff flycatcher. For me that counts as "pending" on the life list, i.e. it's a tick but I'd sure prefer another, better look. I also definitely heard a mountain wren.

The citadel had been my best bet for must-see Andean condors but it was not to be. One black-chested buzzard-eagle hadn't fooled me although I bet the species fools others; as per buzzards in Scotland being "tourist" eagles. Ten lifers for the day was measly for what was virgin territory but I could not have gone all the way to Peru without visiting Machu Picchu. Or hiking part of it.

The last couple of kilometres back were easiest along the railway track plus its tunnels, guarded with "*No Entre*" signs. Screw that: what appeared to be locals in front of me were ignoring them, so I followed suit with a little trepidation. No tunnel was more than an elongated arch but lengthy enough that being caught in the middle with a train bearing down would have needed a scramble to escape. Good thing the line wasn't busy and the few services on it ambled along.

A basic but welcome shower awaited me at my hostel before I mooched around town and ate. I fancied exotic. *The Rough Guide* had described El Indio Feliz as "exceptional for inexpensive prices" but tables needed to be reserved. Not at four o'clock in the afternoon they didn't. I breezed in and enjoyed a plate of the local trout, which was amazing in itself but the trimmings made the dish. Mango, limes, herby crisp-type items and rice all contributed to a culinary experience.

Eat it and die.

Aguas Calientes

Death hadn't arrived the next morning but all was not well. For a start I was itching like buggery. Nasty red welts had appeared on my arms and face. Of course I hadn't bothered to "spray up" post-shower the previous afternoon. I was in town for God's sake. What could possibly bite me there?

Plenty, it turns out. Thereafter almost everywhere I went tourists were divided into those who had visited Machu Picchu, marked by multitudinous bites, and those who hadn't made it there yet – virgin skin.

In addition as the morning progressed, the sky filled with smoke and charred ash began to fall. None of the locals was fazed by these signs of forest fires and the trains kept coming in and going out but I was glad this haze hadn't ruined the views the day before.

On the plus side Tuesday racked up nineteen new species for my life list, largely by the simple expedient of hanging out in the grounds of the Machu Picchu Pueblo Hotel. This is far more upmarket than my sort can afford but we can sneak in and stake out the hummingbird feeders and bananas skewered onto trees for tanagers. It's a birders' paradise targeted on the whole at North Americans, one of whom joined me.

It was hard to keep up with the avian comings and goings and my scribbles of descriptions merged to breed weird hybrids of species that didn't exist. It took a couple of days' untangling to settle on seven or eight tanagers, four hummingbirds, a chlorophonia and a euphonia. Those two are finches but as colourful as the tanagers and worth the trip in themselves.

This was my first introduction to the oropendolas – large birds with outrageous bright yellow undertail feathers. They're related to American blackbirds and orioles and this one, the dusky-green, is the highland representative of a basically Amazonian genus. There would be more in the jungle.

My favourites of the hummers were the local race of collared Inca, with its rusty breast and throat; and one tiny, tiny speckled hummingbird. It's small enough to be the same size as our goldcrest but fully one-sixth of that length is given over to its bill.

In a brief hiatus my co-watcher said, "There's a cock-of-the-rock down by the river. My group saw it earlier."

This is guaranteed to set the pulse racing. Peru's national bird and a bright orange spectacle to boot. When I could tear myself away from the feeders, I went in search but drew a blank. Along with the condor, it was an enigmatic species that eluded me.

Despite the smoke the afternoon train did leave on schedule and my seat-mate this time was an Irishman who'd been at the IMF beano the week before. He was embarrassed by Lima's police overkill and taking the opportunity for a little R&R to make the long flight worthwhile.

We passed one lineside fire as the sky began to clear before the light faded into evening. Approaching Ollantaytambo, a small creature with outrageous tail feathers hovered by our passing train. So insect-like was it that it took me a moment to consider hummingbird, but which one? The field was narrow – a long-tailed sylph or one of two trainbearers. Our elevation was too high and too dry for the sylph and a tad too low for black-tailed trainbearer. Green-tailed was much the most probable species for its characteristics and that's what went into my records. Pending of course but there was no way I was passing up one of South America's specialities.

The Amazon Jungle

Birding took a back seat in favour of washing on my day back in Cusco. It rained in the afternoon anyway, so it passed with a leisurely alpaca steak at Greens Restaurant – another upmarket eaterie. I was developing a taste for them.

The morning after, a cool little British Aerospace jet flew through clouds and mountains down to Puerto Maldonado. The tallest peak I saw, way off to the south, must have been in Bolivia; I like to think so. The snow-clad heights of the Andes gave way to greenery traced through with sandy rivers. Their yellow came across as a mad Fauvist impression of water.

After landing, the open doors of the plane allowed a steaming humidity to seep through the cabin as a preface to the sauna radiating off the tarmac. Having flown with just cabin baggage, as per instructions, I was soon out of the terminal and into an open-sided bus, which would wait for Amazonia guests from two incoming flights. This pause added more blue-grey tanagers and the first turkey vulture of the trip.

The drive away from the airport turned into a tour of the dusty baking town, whose traffic was principally motorbikes and tuk-tuks. The few birds were nothing new but I was more concerned that I'd run out of water and would soon dehydrate into a pile of dust myself. We did finally stop at a cafe, where a Dutch couple and I agreed we were ravenous. With three hours to go before lunch, we piled into hamburgers and sod the advice about not eating local food.

Two of these hours comprised a motorised canoe

trip east and down the Rio Madre de Dios to the lodge. Donning mandatory life-jackets didn't help the sweaty conditions.

Now, this river had 300 miles to meander through Bolivia before joining the Mamoré and becoming the Madeira across Brazil for 700 miles. At which point it merged into the Amazon, which in turn had another 700 miles to reach the sea. So our river must surely have been some tiny, wee tributary?

Well, how can I put this?

The one road crossing at PM had to be half the length of the original Severn Bridge, and that spans two rivers, right at their mouths. Peru's little stream was already as wide as any river in the UK. Moreover, the Tambopata soon joined the Madre de Dios to swell its girth and that's what we chugged down. There was plenty of room to avoid other boats for instance. As per the Severn Estuary, the river had shallows and banks to avoid but these were excellent loafing spots for black skimmers, another cocoi heron and three lifers.

The first of these had to wait weeks after my return to Britain for a positive ID but greater yellow-headed vulture and large-billed tern were unmistakable additions. My new Dutch friend was interested in my sightings so I kept him up to speed on the journey.

Lunch on our arrival was chicken and a whole bunch of stuff wrapped in an apparent vine leaf. It was way too much after the emergency hamburger and sadly went to waste in a great many cases – mine included.

Another lifer, right in the lodge, was a pale-winged trumpeter, which seemed to have adopted the place and even knew how to play pool – the version where pecking balls into pockets counted. This is a bird that's frequently kept as a pet, so tame is it. Closely related to cranes, it's half their size with dark plumage and a prominent white tail-end. We did go on to see wild individuals from one of the trails later in the weekend.

That wasn't the only resident. A scarlet macaw also tended to perch round the guests. If I say it was twice the size of the trumpeter, you have to understand that much consisted of tail. It's nevertheless a big parrot with a striking white face and the scarlet describes most of its body feathers but the wings are a bright blue. This chap could and did fly, so he must have found the lodge easy pickings but a blue-and-yellow macaw had been taken in with a broken wing and was there for life. The two giant parrots were the best of mates and frequently hung out together. It was quite an intimate encounter with two of South America's charismatic species.

EcoAmazonia was a big site with cabins separated from the actual lodge by walkways round squares of gardens and trees. Noisy birds nested here and their calls provided a rainforest backdrop to our meal. At first I took the sounds to be a recording, so westernised am I, but no, we were truly in the Amazon. I couldn't ID the birds to start with, being merely aware of yellow flashes in dark plumage but I sorted out two species eventually. They were yellow-rumped caciques and russet-backed oropendolas. The oropendolas had a stupendous bubbling, cronking song, which put me in mind of the weird Australian currawongs; they were unrelated though, being right up the far end of the passerines among orioles and new world blackbirds, as I wrote when we first met the family.

Our introductory walk was to Caimán Cocha – meaning swamp of the caimans – where twenty or so hoatzins occupied bushes round the fringe. This was one of my target species, simply for its appearance. Imagine a big blue-faced, red-eyed cuckoo with a punk hairdo; imagine Johnny Rotten swaddled in a shaggy brown cloak. Americans will have an easier job of this if they start from their roadrunner. These guys really are dressed up for the party and they do congregate.

More additions to my list were wattled jacanas, the truly slender and narrow-winged fork-tailed palm-swifts and social flycatchers, which I'd sort of logged as one of the kiskadees. Days later I had to admit that these birds lacked the kiskadees' slight yellow crown and brown tones in the wing feathers. So I settled on the flycatchers but I bet I had seen kiskadees.

Oh, and we did see caimans. They came out of the swamp when our guides started making a racket. They were kind of cute – the caimans, that is, not our guides. (OK, they were kind of cute too.) But I wouldn't give much for the life of a caiman: creepy-crawlies creepy-crawled all over them and the sole relief they had was back in the swamp to stick an eye above the surface from time to time. That was eerie, watching those eyes pop up, and blink out of existence again.

While I'm on creatures other than birds, I should mention monkeys: there were plenty of them. And one jaguar poo, but no actual jaguars.

So the end of our first jungle day came to pass and a group of dark, noisy, jeering birds dropped into the camp. Wow, what strange family were they? No more exotic than jays as it turned out. I had them as purplish jays, who are endemic to the Madre de Dios and one of the few corvid species in South America. Violaceous jay is a more widespread cousin and possible in the area but far more... violet, as the name suggests.

The lifers weren't over because a pair of pale-legged horneros became my third ovenbird species and one whose behaviour gives the family its name. They build their dome-shaped mud nests on branches that frequently overhang water. The branches are not necessarily the thickest, so the whole enterprise is a little dodgy.

The day's activities rounded off with a night-time canoe trip out into the river. The boatman killed the engine and we drifted back to the lodge on the current while Ricardo, who was our guide, spun some tale. About what I couldn't say: I was more captivated by unfamiliar stars and fireflies.

Around Madre de Dios

The next morning brought a dilemma. I'd already sweated through one shirt and at that rate I would be out of them by the evening. A foray to Saville Row wasn't on the cards, so something would have to pull double-duty. I folded myself back into the outfit of the day before; I swear it was beginning to stand up on its own. More disgusting was my hat, which was already beginning to smell. This was a new experience; once back in England, the hat went into the first load of washing. I've never washed a hat before.

There was plenty of time before breakfast so I went birding. The very first species was hard to identify but I wasn't that bothered: I'd see it again and again.

Like hell. It was rich rufous on the forehead and underparts and much darker backed. Foraging under the huts, it had to be an antbird – the only one I'm now confident of having seen. Was it in my *Birds of Peru*? Not in all my trawls through its pages. A cursory Web-search on my return to Britain uncovered *nada* until a final concerted effort found a female of a common species – blackish antbird. Common maybe but a huge first for me. However, it's not been recorded in Madre de Dios but the similar black antbird fits the bill there and that's where my record stands.

After breakfast we hiked to Lake Apu Victor – basically a bigger swamp – and Ricardo paddled us round it. We were now old hands at hopping in and out of canoes, so life-jackets were optional, if not actually unavailable. This paddle brought us closer to the previous day's species and close to a bush of farting anis. That's not their full name. My field guide demurely describes one of their calls as a hiss. But it is a fart. We could hear them on this occasion but not see them; that came later. They're a sort of cuckoo and not a million miles away from the hoatzins.

On the return hike we did see one mega, in the guise of a horned screamer. It's another oddity that's lumped in between pheasants and geese and its colouring is similar to a Brent goose. However, it sits on bushes and the first one we saw took off from its perch and lumbered over to a nether region of the marsh to be lost from view. That was frustrating but there was a longer sighting later.

More tantalising was a distant vulture in with the yellow-heads and blacks. It was bigger and had obvious white markings. I tried to put Ricardo on to it but it was gone and he dismissed it as an immature yellow-headed. My scribbled notes mentioned a white leading edge and this fits king vulture, so that's what it became when I found it in the field guide.

I should fill you in on the rest of the crew at this stage. Our guide, Ricardo, you've met and he was a top birder: he could identify species by behaviour, which was crucial for a few flybys. The Dutch couple you also know. Among the other guests were Steve, an American naturalist and tour guide working in Mexico for his own company Mexitreks – neat name. He too knew his birds. With him was Natasha, a delightfully wacky Canadian. By the end of the stay she'd perfected her pale-winged trumpeter impression – a series of hoots rounded off with a deep trill.

Mallory and Katie were a couple of American girls travelling together. Initially I forgot who was who and decided to call them both Katie Mallory but Mallory was the blonde and Katie the dark one. After their three nights in the jungle our paths would recross in Cusco for a "quiet" drink, of which I shall soon tell.

The Seven Guests was the roster for these nights and we all dined together in a little enclave among large gangs of mostly French tourists. And don't get me started on them, ordering huge rounds of cocktails and swamping the bar staff. We were of course much more demure and restrained.

Until it came to the rope swing towards the end of the way back from Apu Victor. I'm ashamed to say that a few of us were immature enough to indulge. Katie and Mallory of course. And Natasha. Even the Dutch guy. And someone else, whose identity I forget now. Moving swiftly on...

Ricardo found a hole by the path, which we would all have ignored. But he broke off a twig and proceeded to thread it gently down the hole.

"A-ha," he grunted as he withdrew the stick, followed by a disturbed tarantula.

"Female," he said.

It may or may not have been to my eyes but she was an impressive hairy beast a few inches across. I'd seen one decades before, ambling in front of me at the Arizona-Sonora Desert Museum, so this wasn't a first. Nevertheless, it kept the exotic wildlife ticking over and marked Ricardo out as a top naturalist.

Continuing along our return, great black hawks were becoming common and macaws flew over from time to time. The screaming theme recurred when another target bird appeared. This was a grey species and nondescript but, like our garden warbler, that is its field mark. A screaming piha – such a fine name – was on the last leg to the lodge. Then came a much more colourful bluish-fronted jacamar with its kingfisher bill and bright green plumage. Our bird was cooperative and sat and let us admire it.

After another shower, lunch and a wee siesta, we hopped back into the motorised canoes for a short haul across the river to Monkey Island. As we left, a small bird clung to a bankside bush; it was streaky, like a sparrow, and may have had a patch of yellow on its face. My description to Ricardo led him to pronounce it as a species of river tyrant. I had to wait for the evening to scan my field guide before logging it as a yellow-browed sparrow, which is similarly common in that habitat.

The island was of course full of monkeys that had been transplanted from places where they were unsafe. They'd either started tame or become that way and scampered down from trees to take proffered bananas. It wasn't quite the thrill of trying to squint at them hiding away up in the branches.

Dozens of black vultures also found the interior of the island to their taste but we had to walk a mile or so back to the river before the birds became numerous. This was as much to do with the trees stopping as anything. The lack of canopy made it easier to see flyovers and among these were blue-headed parrots, probable ruddy pigeons and red-and-green macaws. The wild macaws always seemed to fly in pairs and all their names had to distinguish between what were basically sizeable blue parrots. More confusing was the red-and-green macaw being the same colouring as the scarlet macaw back at the lodge but the green was only conspicuous because it replaced an obvious yellow wing panel on the scarlet macaw. Got that?

Easier to identify was a pair of burrowing owls; for they had been urban residents of Silicon Valley though more than ten years had passed since my previous record. Completely unfazed by our presence, these two sat and blinked in a fallen tree. A bird from another North American family perched nearby, low on a grass stem, which gave me its family straight away: it had to be a blackbird, but an icterid, not our European thrush. With its bright scarlet front it must have been red-breasted blackbird.

This purple patch finished with a wood stork flying the shoreline. By my calculation at that time my world life list stood at 1,197. I wondered which species would take me to 1,200.

A shower was the first essential on returning to the Lodge and a change of clothes would have been nice but I've already alluded to the vast wardrobe needed for that. So, apart from walking outfits having to do double duty, the evening wear would have to be just that... evening wear, every evening, in the hope it didn't suffer the sweaty punishment of the day wear. As a sort of compromise for this outfit I bought an EcoAmazonia t-shirt – one size too large because my tighter shirts wouldn't peel off over sticky skin.

That's too many bodily functions for one short book.

Saturday took us to Lost Cocha. It wasn't so much lost as distant and thus the most gruelling of the outings. The boatman took us farther down river to the start of a trail into the forest. At the end of this was another canoe but oar-propelled this time and Ricardo guided us along a swampy waterway through the jungle.

A large blue kingfisher flashed away ahead of us. Its solid red underparts were obvious enough to make it ringed kingfisher. Now I can bring up a bird deliberately omitted from yesterday's account. At the time, Steve and I agreed that a belted kingfisher had flown across Lake Apu Victor. Problem was: that species is strictly North American, so it could have been Amazon kingfisher. Problem with that was: it's green while belted is blue. We put that down to a trick of the light; the lesser extent of markings underneath had been sufficiently clear for one of belted or Amazon. By the end of the five days we would see so many green and blue kingfishers to make both Amazon and ringed a cert; it was that first one that was puzzling.

1,198 species on the world list. But subsequent research and a couple of splits in the following year meant that the ruddy pigeon of Monkey Island had already been my 1,200th tick. As we saw with the armchair tick of house wren, splitting is common in the IOU taxonomy as DNA analysis reveals subspecies, and sometimes races, to be distinct species in their own right. It's uncommon for lumping, the merging of species, to occur so the total world count keeps going up. In 2025 it stands at 11,113. This excludes 163 now known to be extinct; expect that number to rise.

However, lifer numbers 1,199 and 1,200, as I had them at the time, were birds that those of a certain age will recognise. They have seen old Guinness adds and are immediately an expert in this family. Ricardo called out a white-throated toucan flying across in front of us. By this stage the trees had thinned and the vista was less cluttered.

Even so: "Where? Where?" we cried.

Nevertheless it is a big bird and we all followed it into the crown of a tree and I managed good binocular views of it and... what was that yet more colourful bird on the branch below it? Only a chestnut-eared aracari, that was all – another type of toucan. Two in the space of a minute and that was it for our encounter with this iconic Amazonian family.

We were quite heady and not just from the birds. Out in the open the sun was brutal and the channel we were paddling went on and on. And apparently it wasn't the Lost Cocha because at the end of it a short walk took us to a third canoe and a far more overgrown sliver of water. This time the boat needed extra paddling to steer us round tight bends – extra steering from the front and guess who found himself in that position?

My one experience of piloting watercraft was the pedalos at Weston-super-Mare, so my initial efforts were restricted to pushing the canoe off banks we'd ploughed into. I began to get the hang of it and by the return journey could angle my oar in the right direction four times out of five.

It was huge fun. That and the rope swing, I was living my second childhood. What would be next? You'll find out.

Meanwhile exotic species kept coming. As we rounded one bend, a pair of birds reared off the surface of the swamp and splashed away to safety. There was an impression of stripiness, which immediately put me in mind of juvenile great crested grebes. I wasn't a million miles away although this species is not related to the Podicipediformes: it's closer to crakes and rails. It is called a sungrebe and the stripes are restricted to its head but this is most often all that shows while it's on the water. We saw plenty more of these but they never failed to entrance.

Another submarine species was anhinga. This is related to our cormorant but with a much thinner neck, along the lines of the Australian darter. All I saw of it was this neck and upturned bill sinking into the water but the bird was unmistakable. We next earned a proper view of anis by sneaking up on them.

Landfall led to another short walk and a tall observation tower. At last a chance at the canopy species. A pair of thrush-like wrens were nesting in the roof of the tower, so I had cracking views of them but late morning proved to be poor for all else. One tiny yellowish bird with a dark cap, mask and tertial tips was the sole reward and again I had to return to the lodge before identifying it as a yellow-browed tody-flycatcher.

A long walk back in the draining heat was enlivened when Ricardo stopped under a tree and looked up. We all looked up. Yup, tree with branches etc, seen that before. But he told us to look closer and eventually had to point out a great potoo blending motionless into the trunk. This is a daytime trick of the nightjar family, to which potoos are related.

Noted as uncommon in my field guide, it was not at all on my radar and the hardest bird I saw on the entire holiday. It was the eighth lifer of the day, which was kind of slow going, especially when compared with the ten I added back at the lodge that afternoon. These included Manu parrotlet, speckled chachalaca, red-capped cardinal and silver-beaked tanager. That was time off well spent after the exertions of the Lost Cocha.

The Seven Guests were all fit for their final meal together: the Dutch couple and Katie/Mallory were off early next morning to catch their flights back to Cusco. Or so Katie and Mallory thought.

My night in my wee hut was full of drama. Despite one's best efforts insects will enter the rooms and a couple shared my space that Saturday. They weren't over-freaky to start with and one was beautiful with bright green headlamps for eyes. Seriously. When my lights went off, this tiny critter shone his beams and skittered around the floor like a disco ball.

He was clearly harmless and an exhausted sleep descended until the small hours when a clattering and scrabbling woke me. I was discombobulated and it was horror-film dark. But I frighten myself rather more with how cool I am. I clicked on the old iPhone and established that nothing of Dracula proportions was in the vicinity before fishing out my torch. This revealed my glasses on the floor, i.e. not where I'd left them on the bedside cabinet.

A creature the size of a mouse could have done that but the scariness wasn't over yet. A red sticky blob had appeared on my sheet and it was spreading and sinking into the fabric. Was I bleeding? A quick check passed me fit but it did take a while to go back to sleep. By morning the stain had disappeared and it was easy to dismiss the whole episode as a dream.

Being on the lodge's EcoParaiso package (i.e. the whole five days), Ricardo, Steve, Natasha and I went fishing with our boatman on Sunday. Hugging the bank, our canoe motored up the Madre de Dios, which allowed views of spotted sandpiper, striated heron and roadside hawk. Only the latter was a lifer because the sandpiper is a winter visitor from North America and I'd first seen the heron at Port Kelang. That's in Malaysia, so the bird is one widespread species.

So widespread that the IOU have now split the subspecies in the rest of the world off into what they've called little heron. The South American bird gets to keep the original name. That seems like the tail wagging the dog but I'm no phylogenetic expert. I am glad of a further armchair tick.

Our goal was a tributary of the river, and too narrow for our long canoe and its powerful motor, so we careened from side to side in our passage to where the angling could occur. This thrilled me not at all despite the quarry being piranha: I'd have preferred simply to see one. It also confirmed my suspicion that fishing is work, and boring work at that. Ricardo landed one catfish, the boatman the odd tiddler and us gringos drew blanks, which was a relief to me.

However, Spix's guans, and flyover yellow-tufted woodpeckers and black-tailed trogon kept the life list ticking over. Not great views of them except for the canopy-dwelling guans, which are lowland cousins of Andean guan but with a larger and more obvious red wattle.

Eventually bored with fishing, Ricardo and the boatman elected to paddle our canoe, as the easier option, back to the Madre de Dios. This could have accounted for better birding on the return. One hummingbird, which had to be a kind of hermit from the decurved bill, defied clear identification despite the remainder of my notes. Research back in England helped me decide that the obvious red bill and dark undertail had to be long-tailed hermit. This has never been reported on eBird for the region but just the one photo online of a white-bearded hermit matches my notes and leaves it as the best candidate.

A large-headed flatbill was even less certain: my scribbles included brown somewhere on its back, which fits the species. However, the extent and paleness of its yellow throat suggested yellow-breasted flycatcher. Initially the flatbill lost out as it prefers bamboo and we weren't in that part of the forest. The flycatcher though fares worse by the entire absence of eBird records for Madre de Dios. OK, no bamboo but also no suggestion that the species sticks to the one patch for its entire life and it can therefore travel between them. It has also been noted in the area of our travel. It wins.

One species wasn't a problem: I'd already noted white-rumped birds flying up from treetops, without clearer views, but now they were distinctly bat-like. Later I married these two characteristics to narrow the field down to swallow-winged puffbird. You see how the process works? In the mould of Sherlock

Holmes, one eliminates the impossible to arrive at what's hopefully not improbable.

Back at EcoAmazonia another huge lunch and siesta preceded a walk through its botanic garden, where a territorial pale-winged trumpeter rushed us. Natasha took cover behind Steve but continued to perfect her trumpeter calls. Happy with his display of bravado, the bird left us alone and returned to pecking the earth being disturbed by men working the garden.

The lifers kept coming: a splendid blue-crowned motmot, similar, and closely related, to a bee-eater but with an outrageously long tail; cobalt-winged parakeets and a blue dacnis, which wasn't blue at all, but green, being a female. The dacnis is another type of tanager – along with conebills, flowerpiercers and sierra finches – so this one was my 17th of the trip. They're confined to the Americas but confined is hardly the right word for a family that's nearly 400 strong.

Ricardo's catfish was the centrepiece of Sunday dinner. We each had a mouthful and jolly tasty it was. A few beers helped me drop off to sleep despite the previous night's adventure and, besides, there was no repeat.

Back to a Cusco Evening

Leaving the jungle on Monday could have been an anticlimax but our early morning canoe run up the Madre de Dios did provide a couple of lifers. I now decided that the short-tailed bat-like parrots I'd been seeing were mealy amazons. Then among the fork-tailed palm-swifts was a larger individual with a pale neck ring; this had to be a white-collared swift, first seen in Cusco. And my second life tick was collared plover. Collars were in fashion.

We disembarked and the open-sided bus ran us through Puerto Maldonado to the airport and I kept on logging new species. Grey-breasted martin and a bird trailing extensive tail feathers, which must be fork-tailed flycatcher in that part of the world.

Our human flying was becoming wonky at this stage. My own StarPeru flight to Cusco was fine but unexpected at the check-in queue were Mallory and Katie. Avianca had cancelled their departure the day before, put them in a hotel overnight and the girls would in fact be taking off after me. We had a moment to confirm our date in town that evening before my wee jet was whisking me back over the jungle and into the snow-clad mountains and I landed back up at 11,000 feet.

How long does it take altitude acclimatisation to wear off? Not long, I can tell you. Not willing to pay 30 soles for a taxi from the airport, I walked out to hail one on the highway, except they were thin on the ground and I ended up hiking a mile or so. Up hill. With a backpack – albeit small and light.

Boy, was I whacked by the time I scrambled into a

cab, but the fare of a mere cinco soles was validation for suffering such exertion. I had to spend the rest of the afternoon in recovery back at my hotel, which was becoming home from home. It may have attracted a few negative comments from the over-privileged on TripAdvisor but they need to realise that Peru is by no means a rich country, nor one with a modern infrastructure. The people battle along as they can and they do a bloody good job, apart from being gentle and helpful with it. So it was with the Monte Horeb staff; they made my stay a pleasure.

So, that Monday evening in Cusco was... what? It started quietly in Paddy's, on the corner of Plaza de Armas and thus the "highest Irish-owned pub in the world". A pint went down while waiting for Mallory and Katie. I began to fear they'd be a no-show but, half an hour late, in they breezed and dragged me off to the launderette to collect their washing. Of course the poor girls had had to compress two days into a mere few hours before they travelled down to Lake Titicaca.

We repaired to their hostel, which was truly Back-packer Central and way out of my ken. This was basically a bar belting out music with accommodation for that little window between closing time and breakfast. Here, American, Australian and Kiwi kids crossed paths on their exotic itineraries round South America and swapped tales of amazement and awe-someness. To think, at their age I viewed France as just a little closer than Jupiter.

The girls and I and sundry companions drank Cus-queñas, played cards and pisco sours began to fill the table. I remember gazing across a sea of them and then...

It was Tuesday morning and by a miracle I was in bed, at Monte Horeb. I floated up and out for a hearty breakfast. This alone should have told me I was still pissed, and in a strange and alien way. But I was loving Peru and its people and even the taxi back to the airport. A 25-minute wait on the runway for congestion to ease at Lima couldn't dampen my enthusiasm either.

We eventually flew back along the ridge of the Andes and down into the aridity. I kept expecting to see Machu Picchu one last time from the air but all the folds of the hills and valleys merged into one and I couldn't tell you which route we took.

My cab was waiting at Lima and the journey back to Miraflores was the terminal challenge to my constitution. I could face nothing but bed back at Hostal el Patio and so my last full day on Peruvian soil dawned.

Lima Redux

Pantanos de Villa had been on my radar since arriving in Peru so an entire day turned into the perfect opportunity to visit. It's a Ramsar site, which means it should be perfect for waterbirds but it was a tad too far to walk. A taxi for the morning would have cost me $50 and would have been worth it in the event but... if there's a public transport option, I'll take it and I'd got wind of a well-kept Lima secret – to whit, the Metropolitano.

This is a proper bus service with a proper timetable on its own tracks, not like the battered collectivos, which must take a couple of years to fathom. It runs as far south as Chorrillos and I figured that Pantanos was a mile or so on from there.

That final leg was not so simple and began to take me into what might be described as the barrios. The first symptom of these was the preponderance of dog shit on the pavements. The buildings became ever more precarious, clinging to hillsides and towering above each other. The needs of the motor car dominated local businesses: such dirty deeds were not fit for genteel neighbourhoods. It was sad to see this demographic reduced to servicing the Machine.

On the plus side, my route skirted the first of ponds that a taxi would have rushed past, and white-cheeked pintail and Andean coot started a new batch of lifers; they were a double plus because they weren't on the main reserve. A couple of ospreys were also one-off sightings.

Time was ticking away and it was heading for the afternoon lull when I reached the reserve entrance. I paid my fee, plied a trail or two and met groups of excited Peruvian schoolchildren, who were keen to practise their English on me, usually at the tops of their voices. So, about the only new species during this phase was grassland yellow finch; it could have been Raimondi's yellow finch, they're so similar but I had to pick one and the eBird favourite won out.

Two herons rounded the day off. One was small and therefore least bittern. Its identification was so easy, I couldn't believe it was a lifer. A summer visitor to both California and the east coast of the USA, it had eluded my years there as a resident. The second species had been a tentative record in Alviso, at the foot of San Francisco Bay; this time it was an obvious little blue heron strutting at the far side of one pool. That would have been it but a later check of my notes revealed that one gull I'd identified as a juvenile grey-headed must have been an adult Franklin's, so the haul for a rather urban part of Lima was 22 species.

Overnight flights west to east are a pain in the arse. You might think you have all day on foreign soil to soak up its final glories but in reality the axeman of a missed flight is forever looming. I walked hither and thither in Miraflores and took in the department stores with their Christmas displays, complete with snow. By mid-afternoon though I was glad to be back in the taxi and heading for Jorge Chavez airport.

There my remaining soles stretched to a snack and a beer but not a bottle of water, so I bought chewy sweeties for the flight.

The plane taxied out to the runway and fired up its engines.

Or at least tried to. A couple of attempts later the captain came on and explained that the starter motor had failed and he was sending to the terminal for another one. This duly arrived and all systems were go but it begged the question of what would happen in mid-flight or on landing when reverse thrust was needed. The seasoned traveller in me dismissed these thoughts and I enjoyed one forgettable movie and a welcome rerun of *Little Miss Sunshine*.

Our red-eye landed in Madrid on time despite the delay and we engine-braked to a halt in fine style. And 4€ was sufficient for the Metro to my hotel on Avenida de América.

The Big Month

Despite having missed a night's sleep and needing the comfort of the upmarket Abba Hotel, I partook of the local area and recognised it as the posh shops I'd seen back in 2004. I enjoyed a couple of fabulous bars and their tapas before tiredness did overtake me.

The next day's flight back to Bristol should have been a cinch but queues at the EasyJet check-in were horrendous; I was back to cattle class. The rest of the procedure was then a hurry, so of course security was ultra-fussy. Perhaps they'd sussed I'd been to South America. However, I've never missed a plane and I didn't miss this one.

Persistent rain greeted me on touchdown and I was back to reality and my first day in an unfurnished flat. Yes, my life had contrived to overlap the trip with a move from the centre of Bristol to Clevedon and my time was full with teething troubles.

So, by the next weekend I had no idea what the trip count was or, more important for the last day of October, what my month list was. I'd expected that with such a huge bird list Peru would make it a shoe-in for my best ever, which stood at 257. That March 2009 count included New Zealand, California and good old Blighty. I'd identified fewer species than anticipated in Peru but felt that a little effort would break the record, so I started close to my new home, at the coast by Dowlais Farm. This brought singing skylarks, stonechats, rock pipits and a reed bunting among the usual suspects.

Next had to be Blagdon Lake, especially because of a reported Bewick's swan, which wasn't there, but three black-necked grebes were. Most unexpected was a sole golden plover in with the lapwing flock. Not only was this new for the month but new for my Avon list.

The Stratford Hide at Chew Valley was next but signs declared it to be out of operation. That was why the car park was so empty. But I'd already decanted scope, boots and God knows what else from the car, so... I went in. My reward at the perfectly OK hide was my 203rd Avon species with bearded tits pinging in the nearby reedbed. How often had I missed them? Often enough obviously. An omission that continues to this day. How is it that everyone else sees them?

I worked the rest of the lake and went home to tally the month. The result came to 257 – a dead heat. One extra species would beat the record but where? With dusk approaching the most obvious target was a glossy ibis at Pilning Wetland in South Gloucestershire. The bird was big enough and, besides, other site regulars might do the job.

Despite hammering up the M5 and half-running to the scrapes and reedbeds, bugger all showed until a lone water rail squealed for month bird number 258. Moreover, it was new for my Pilning list and therefore not one of the regulars.

Ironic therefore that a Twitter post later in the evening mentioned a red-crested pochard at Chew Valley, which I'd omitted to log despite being my first one there. I'd been on 258 all along and had therefore hit 259 for the month.

The lifers, and month birds, weren't over: my notebook contained unidentified scribbled descriptions and sketches. With an Internet of trip reports to trawl through, I would nail some of these mysteries. For example, the cliff flycatcher coming down off Machu Picchu was one such.

Another, dark brown-rumped species, suggested black-capped donacobius. It didn't fit but Web pictures of a donacobius showed a yellowish tinge to the belly that my field guide didn't. A synapse must have fired because I leafed back through the abandoned and crossed out sketches, and one was a perfect fit. It was the first of the mystery birds on the canoe out of Puerto Maldonado and therefore my first lifer in the Amazon. Later, Ricardo would allude to hearing the species and I would conclude that maybe I too had heard its weird duet.

Another Amazonian lifer nailed in this debriefing was the white-bearded hermit to bring me up to 263 (by the 2024 taxonomy) and there I fear it must stay. Too much time has passed for further detective work. However, if there is a next time, I'll be much better armed.

The Peru List

174 species according to the 2024 IOU taxonomy:

06 Oct   Hostal el Patio: West Peruvian Dove
                        Scrub Blackbird
            Parque 7 de Junio:
                        Amazilia Hummingbird
                        Feral Pigeon
                        Harris's Hawk
                        Southern Beardless Tyrannulet
                        Vermilion Flycatcher
                        Southern House Wren
                        Long-tailed Mockingbird
                        Bananaquit
                        Saffron Finch
            Miraflores: Eared Dove
                        Red-masked Parakeet
                        White-crested Elaenia
                        Tropical Kingbird
                        Rufous-collared Sparrow
                        Shiny Cowbird
            Lima Coast: Belcher's Gull
                        Kelp Gull
                        Inca Tern
                        Peruvian Booby
                        Neotropic Cormorant
                        Peruvian Pelican
                        Black Vulture
            Larco Mar: American Kestrel
                        Blue-grey Tanager

07 Oct	Lima:	Peregrine Falcon
		Blue-black Grassquit
	El Olivar:	House Sparrow
	Huaca Pucllana:	
		Croaking Ground Dove
		White-winged Parakeet
	Lima Coast:	Blackish Oystercatcher
08 Oct	Plaza San Francisco:	Chiguanco Thrush
		Peruvian Sierra Finch
	Plaza de Armas:	Giant Hummingbird
09 Oct	Plaza de Armas:	Hooded Siskin
		Golden-billed Saltator
	Sacsayhuaman:	Bare-faced Ground Dove
10 Oct	Rio Saphi:	Puna Ibis
		Black-chested Buzzard-Eagle
	Sacsayhuaman:	Chestnut-breasted Coronet
		Creamy-crested Spinetail
		Cinereous Conebill
		Band-tailed Seedeater
		Black-throated Flowerpiercer
	Plaza de Armas:	White-collared Swift
11 Oct	Poroy-Anta train:	Cattle Egret
		Cocoi Heron
	Urubamba:	Torrent Duck
		Andean Gull
		Black Phoebe
	Aguas Calientes:	
		Green-and-white Hummingbird
		Torrent Tyrannulet
		Blue-and-white Swallow
12 Oct	Machu Picchu:	Andean Guan
		White-tipped Swift
		Streaked Xenops
		Sierran Elaenia
		Tufted Tit-Tyrant
		Mountain Wren

Slate-throated Whitestart
Spectacled Whitestart
Blue-necked Tanager
Urubamba: Cliff Flycatcher
13 Oct Aguas Calientes: Lesser Violetear
Speckled Hummingbird
Collared Inca
Variable Hawk
Mitred Parakeet
Sclater's Tyrannulet
Grey-breasted Wood Wren
White-capped Dipper
Blue-naped Chlorophonia
Thick-billed Euphonia
Common Bush Tanager
Dusky-green Oropendola
Rust-and-yellow Tanager
Masked Flowerpiercer
Blue-and-yellow Tanager
Blue-capped Tanager
Golden-naped Tanager
Silver-backed Tanager
Urubamba: Green-tailed Trainbearer
15 Oct Puerto Maldonado: Turkey Vulture
Black-capped Donacobius
Palm Tanager
Madre de Dios: Solitary Sandpiper
Black Skimmer
Large-billed Tern
Greater Yellow-headed Vulture
Eco Amazonia: Pale-winged Trumpeter
Rose-fronted Parakeet
Scarlet Macaw
Russet-backed Oropendola
Yellow-rumped Cacique
Giant Cowbird

Caimán Cocha: Fork-tailed Palm Swift
                Wattled Jacana
                Hoatzin
                Social Flycatcher
Eco Amazonia: Black-fronted Nunbird
                Lineated Woodpecker
                Pale-legged Hornero
                Purplish Jay
16 Oct   Eco Amazonia: Blackish Antbird
                Plumbeous Kite
                White-eyed Parakeet
                Eastern Wood Pewee
Lake Apu Victor: Horned Screamer
                Greater Ani
                King Vulture
                Great Black Hawk
                Amazon Kingfisher
                Bluish-fronted Jacamar
                Blue-and-yellow Macaw
                Screaming Piha
Eco Amazonia: Yellow-browed Sparrow
Monkey Island: Ruddy Pigeon
                Wood Stork
                Burrowing Owl
                Blue-headed Parrot
                Red-and-green Macaw
                Red-breasted Blackbird
17 Oct   Lost Cocha: Great Potoo
                Sungrebe
                Anhinga
                Ringed Kingfisher
                Chestnut-eared Aracari
                White-throated Toucan
                Yellow-browed Tody-Flycatcher
                Thrush-like Wren

Eco Amazonia: Speckled Chachalaca
Pale-vented Pigeon
Manu Parrotlet
Drab Water Tyrant
Eastern Kingbird
White-banded Swallow
Southern Rough-winged Swallow
Black-billed Thrush
Silver-beaked Tanager
Red-capped Cardinal

18 Oct   Madre de Dios: Spix's Guan
White-bearded Hermit
Spotted Sandpiper
Striated Heron
Great Egret
Roadside Hawk
Black-tailed Trogon
Swallow-winged Puffbird
Yellow-tufted Woodpecker
Large-headed Flatbill
Eco Amazonia: Amazonian Motmot
Cobalt-winged Parakeet
Blue Dacnis

19 Oct   Eco Amazonia: Mealy Amazon
Madre de Dios: Collared Plover
Snowy Egret
Puerto Maldonado:
Fork-tailed Flycatcher
Grey-breasted Martin
Barn Swallow

21 Oct   Pantanos de Villa:
Cinnamon Teal
White-cheeked Pintail
American Moorhen
Andean Coot
Pied-billed Grebe

Great Grebe
Black-necked Stilt
Grey-headed Gull
Franklin's Gull
Least Bittern
Black-crowned Night Heron
Little Blue Heron
Osprey
Grassland Yellow Finch

Tenerife, 2013

Populated by the cast of *Benidorm*, Los Cristianos is as far south as ex-pat Brits venture in Europe. In truth it's as far south as Europe gets. Four hours straight down from Bristol, it offers 20-25°C in November. This was a lot different to the forecast at home for the next few days.

Los Cristianos offers dryness into the bargain, being in the rain shadow of Mount Teide, Spain's highest point. It's one hell of a mountain, thrusting 12,000 feet out of the Atlantic so, yes, it's a volcano. The landscape around provides evidence with its jagged sculpture of mad peaks and ridges.

Dramatic though the terrain is, that's not what lured me. That was pelagic trips out of Los Cristianos but the time of year was all wrong for seabirds. I'd give the ferry to La Gomera a whirl but with the underwhelming expectation of a nice ride. No matter: the Canary Islands have endemics and I'm all for endemics.

I'd need a car for them but I had a few days on foot first. That didn't stop my world list since a local species was a short climb out of the resort. My slog up the parched scrub of Montaña de Guaza intended to find overwintering warblers. Sardinian were likely but spectacled were also possible. A couple of buzzy calls on the way up could have been either but they flew my mind when I found a route along the top of cliffs.

These ran to the south of the resort and earlier a large falcon had glided in and perched. It was probably a peregrine but round those parts the North

African Barbary falcon is an equal candidate. The bird's plumage from above would settle it, so that became my quarry.

You can guess there was no other sighting. But my lifer was up there – several of them – confiding as they furtled around the scrub. Berthelot's pipit lives and breeds on the Canary Islands and Madeira so it's close to endemic. The odd meadow pipit can pass through so identification was necessary but easy: the native bird has bold face markings and is a sandy grey – job done.

It was a surprise so close to Los Cristianos. Less surprising all over the place were Iberian chiffchaffs with their squeaky calls. The slim town-centre roster was completed by collared doves and... Spanish sparrows in Spain. (I'd seen them in Venice.) I hadn't realised that most sparrows moult into a winter plumage so these birds weren't in their resplendent black streaks. Instead the males sported more subdued necklaces but those did separate them from house sparrows.

The latter must have been in town: they're all over the world. But I wasn't going to bust a gut to find them; likewise for the African collared doves that are supposed to have escaped captivity. One or two of the feral pigeons were candidates for pure rock doves; one well-marked individual up on the cliffs had to have been an original.

The harbour added yellow-legged and lesser black-backed gulls. Diligent searching added little egret, grey wagtails and turnstones – that far south!

After this initial foray my field guide corrected me on one fundamental point: Los Cristianos' Iberian chiffchaffs are not a subspecies; they are an entirely distinct species, endemic to the Canaries, and in hindsight my first lifer of the holiday. I was identifying them by location but my *Collins* described one song I'd heard and puzzled over. Similar to the Cetti's chatter, it was noticeable as being way out of place in a manicured metropolis. The source was this Canary Islands chiffchaff and I was happy with that.

Otherwise, my holiday started true to form with me in the worst of health. I'd been coughing like a bastard for two weeks previously, violently enough to tear stomach muscles, for which I was taking pain-killers. That's not something I readily do.

On day three the remnants of the cough became a raging sore throat – sufficient to submit myself to a pharmacy. The lady there was *muy* charming but must have seen me coming. When I tried to translate the text on her cure's packaging back in my hotel room, even my Spanish was up to recognising the word homoeopathic.

I'd used that snake oil before but... oh well, it would have been a waste of euros otherwise. And a few hours later I had to admit how effective it was. I was sufficiently well to sit in a bar and watch the Germans hand us a friendly football lesson at Wembley. Poor old Adam Lallana: his first two England outings ended in defeat. At the time I hoped it wouldn't tarnish one of the nation's best prospects for a while. Now he's left Southampton and I don't care.

Don't be fooled by how cheap the crossing from Los Cristianos to the smaller island of La Gomera appears to be. A big sign in the Armas ferry terminal adver-tised a ticket from 11.50€. From – that's what *desde* means in my Spanish dictionary. At the time I wasn't at all discombobulated to be charged 27€ for a return journey: the extra 4€ were clearly down to some dis-qualification from the basic fare. At my age, marital status and ethnicity I'm used to that.

The 40-kilometre trip (about the distance between Dover and Calais – foot passenger day return £25) supplied a few Cory's shearwaters. They started not far from Tenerife and within range of the whale-watching boats, so the ferry might not have been necessary. They were nearly a lifer: I'd only ever seen them in 1997 from the QE2 on the way back from New York.

The landing point is San Sebastián de La Gomera, clinging to another lump of volcanic rock. It's an unprepossessing town but plain swifts greeted me for a kosher lifer. I'd understood them to be widespread on Tenerife but these proved to be my one encounter, which sugared the Gomera pill.

In fairness the island's attraction lies up, in its rainforest, and needs more than a couple of hours to appreciate. A couple of days would be more suitable. My time allowed one brief stroll, which produced no more birds so I returned to the ferry where the stewardess wouldn't let me on with my "return" ticket.

Our inter-lingual gymnastics, as she was distracted with other passengers, established that my already bloated 27€ had merely permitted me thus far. The stark choice was buying another ticket to return me to my bed for the night or arguing in the quarter hour before departure to face an additional hotel bill while cooling my heels for the next day's boat. A nearby couple of burly uniforms intimated that discretion was the best course and I half-ran back to the Armas office.

Where a further 23€ was a strange amount for the missing part of my ticket and made a total fare of 50€. That was £42 in proper money, for a one-hour crossing – a pricey trip, but the going rate for a non-resident, I later learned.

I scurried back in time for the the ferry and on the

return crossing simply watched as Tenerife loomed larger. An obvious scar marked the earthworks, tunnels and bridges of the new motorway from Adeje to Santiago del Teide.

But no traffic. The road had been in completion for a long, long time and one of the ferry hands assured me it would be ready next year. It matched the undeveloped, but bulldozed, tracts of land all around Los Cristianos. Clearly the collapse of Spain overtook all these projects. The road did open at the end of 2015, probably financed by an austerity imposed on the ordinary Spaniard.

Public transport on the Canaries suffers an even worse deal, so by Thursday a car would have to unlock my remaining Tenerife goals. Any old junk on wheels would do and that's what I got – a Tata. As long as it went up hills I didn't care and the first hill on the itinerary was Mount Teide itself. Not right to the top of the volcano. Only the cable car does that but a climb of 7,000 feet up one flank was necessary for Las Lajas picnic site.

This height was sufficient to be in the cloud base and a thin mist wafted hither and thither, and a chill meant that I did need my fleece. I wondered if conditions were right for the location's renowned star turn. However, the endemic blue chaffinch (*Fringilla teydea*) was the first bird to show, right by the toilets – one of those habitats that birders get to know. A dripping tap was the real attraction and the bird permitted splendid views as it sipped from the puddle beneath.

Larger than our common chaffinch, the male is naturally a pale blue all over; the female is a uniform grey and harder to distinguish from *Fringilla coelebs*. My bird was an easy male for lifer number 1,080. (Bearing in mind the caveat about subsequent splits and lumps, alluded to in Peru.)

More puzzling was a yellowish finch that perched and sang openly and made me wonder if it were siskin or serin. It was rather plain and didn't answer for either bird. This is where birders, who know of so many species, can be too smart for their own good.

Ask a layman what they might expect in the Canaries and they'd say... what would they say? Come on, the clue's in the name – Canary Islands. Geddit?

Yeah, I didn't get it until I consulted *Collins* and then– goddammit, was the bird streaky or not? By now it had disappeared and half an hour passed before another individual perched, sang with gay abandon and confirmed that it was indeed a canary. Endemic to the Atlantic islands, the species does occur on Madeira but that didn't matter for the pipit and they both count as a Tenerife speciality.

In the meantime my third lifer of the day had been more obvious. A dark-capped blue tit lived up to the description for African blue tit. The name tells us this is not endemic but the Canaries have several of their own subspecies (with no wing bar). This one is *Cyanistes teneriffae teneriffae* and one day a split may happen...

The mist was turning into a fog. I'd noticed how Teide acquired a cap of clouds as the day progressed and I was right in it. So, leaving Las Lajas, my route continued not much higher to a flank where the most recent major eruption (1798) had left fields of lava and blackened rubble with one bizarre lone tree in the middle of the blasted landscape. The road ran on down a broad valley to Guia de Isora where I encountered the only ravens of the trip – the only corvids in fact. The Canaries has a dearth of them with not so much as a crow, jackdaw or magpie.

My list was running at six lifers in five days and I'd

basically hit most of my target species (plus one). The next two – pigeons that inhabit the northern slopes and show early in the day – would be more of a challenge.

My second day with the car took me to their favoured spot at Las Grimonas viewpoint, across the west side of Tenerife. This involved an early start for two reasons: first, the roads past Adeje were slower thanks to the missing motorway to Santiago del Teide, where they twisted over a spur of the volcano; second, I now understood that my targets were active until the sun shone on their cliff face. Which wouldn't be a problem: late November, the sun doesn't rise far enough to shine on that steep slope.

The viewpoint was a lay-by off a busy coastal highway and intended for gazers out across the sea. We birders, however, turned inwards and up to a vista that wasn't at all what I was expecting. Described as one of the last patches of laurel forest, the habitat must be truly screwed. The odd tree clung to a scrubby precipice above the road.

This did narrow down where I needed to look. Better yet, the first candidate for my pigeons flapped into what must have been one of the laurels as I got out of the car. There wasn't even time to slip into my binoculars' strap as I swung them on to the bird. Tail pattern is helpful for pigeon identification in general and, following it from below, easy to register. My individual showed dark, light, dark.

I didn't consult *Collins* right away because watching and absorbing detail was more important but I mentally ticked off laurel pigeon, having understood it to be the most likely. Further detail though was not forthcoming as the bird magically vanished into foliage and during the next 15 minutes the odd rock dove flew out and back, to keep me honest and on my toes.

Two or three kestrels also patrolled the cliff, but nowt else. It was time to confirm my sighting.

It wasn't laurel but Bolle's pigeon, which is slightly the more numerous. Smaller than our wood pigeon, it's more akin to stock dove but without the dark edges to its wings. None of these details was obvious from the glimpse I'd had.

Now it remained to register the pale terminal band that identifies laurel pigeon. Another quarter hour, and maybe a couple of different kestrels, brought it as two individuals flew the length of the cliff. Subtler field marks, such as their larger size and darker hue, eluded me. But, hey, there was no doubt that my world list had moved on to 1,084 and I'd bagged all the Tenerife endemics.

What could I do next?

First was to take in the view from the top of this precipice. The map marked it as scenic, so I drove more wiggly, windy roads to Icod el Alto, 500 metres above Las Grimonas. The sheer drop was vertiginous and hectares of orchards beneath looked like cabbages planted in fields. Matchbox cars beetled along the ribbon of motorway. A lone kestrel went about its business an unfathomable distance below.

Driving on to Teno cliffs, farther west, could have led to Barbary falcon. Once more, Spain's decline was apparent as the road to Punta Teno was closed.

Two that remained open took me over to, and out of, the tourist trap of Masca. Surely built against all the odds, the latter road was a series of crazy hairpins twisting hundreds of metres up and back to Santiago del Teide. I had the surreal experience of following coaches up it – mind you, special short wheelbase coaches. Regardless, a kind of mania must have held for the road to exist, though the territory it crosses is spectacular.

And the kestrels kept coming and they did it all: they soared like sparrowhawks; they perched; they caught insects as per hobbies; they flew in small parties; they called. About the only behaviour I didn't see was their trademark hovering.

At El Fraile on the Saturday, one kestrel did its cactus-sitting thing – another new one on me. It was in a patch of scrub outside an immigrant town, servicing the surrounding tourist traps in south-east Tenerife. Spain's boom years had birthed it and the collapse years will put it first in the tits-up queue as the country's economy worsens.

In the same area a great grey shrike was my reward for visiting and... why isn't that a raptor? It can catch birds along with its preferred prey of rodents. In both cases it impales the victim in its larder of thorns or barbed wire. This is not showmanship: the shrike is poorly equipped for ripping flesh to shreds and needs the "larder" to help. This could be its disqualification from raptorship.

The day seemed to exhaust my birding luck. I'd had eight lifers out of seven attempted, and all the Tenerife endemics. What was left were Barbary partridge and spectacled warbler in this corner of the island. The jury is out on whether the partridges found their own way to the Canaries or were introduced but, similar to the British family members, they are self-sustaining and a kosher tick.

Hence my visit to El Fraile and a nearby pond, at Las Chafiras, where spoonbills were the stars. The supporting cast were common sandpiper and a sleeping greenshank. They were so camouflaged against the soil, I could have missed them without diligent scanning.

I take no credit for finding these sites. An excellent PDF of a 2012 trip by Stewart Betts and Chris Small was a reliable guide and almost up to date. In the intervening year the aforementioned road to Punta Teno had closed and the area round Golf del Sur must have changed because I couldn't find anywhere to park. Was I even in the right place?

I was, because another attempt on the Sunday saw me dump the car and walk in as per instructions. By now I'd memorised the field marks for separating Barbary from red-legged partridge – all fairly subtle and matters of degree but all adding up to a different species. This was to no avail. Sure, birds of their ilk did appear and immediately flew. Away. So the view was of disappearing rumps and from that angle the two species are the same.

After trying to track them down in the desert-like scrub, I resorted to taking their identification as a matter of faith. This was not the first such addition to my 1,085-strong world list.

One further raptor surprised me in the afternoon after I'd returned the car to Playa de las Americas; with plenty of time to kill I elected to walk the couple of miles back to Los Cristianos. Halfway along, what first appeared to be a buzzard laboured over the shoreline – unusual behaviour. For a buzzard. But not so much for an osprey, as my binoculars revealed. We up north associate the bird with lakes and rivers and not the sea, an altogether rougher environment.

This one spent an age soaring and scanning and I'd about had my fill when it dived. Right into the surf. This looked foolhardy.

It thrashed for a moment before its massive wings beat it away from the waves. I'd stopped breathing. The bird shook itself and continued to climb, with a sizeable fish in its talons.

This caught the attention of a yellow-legged gull, which harassed the osprey. I willed the raptor to hold on to its lunch while it manoeuvred the fish into "torpedo" position. As I watched this pursuit into the distance, the osprey saw off the gull and a momentary appearance by a kestrel, tiny in comparison and trying its piracy act on far too big a victim.

That was about it for Tenerife. I returned to the same spot the next day and found a ringed plover. A whimbrel in the evening below the Los Cristianos cliffs finished off the trip list but not the drama.

Cory's shearwaters were the principals of the final Tenerife show, in a way I couldn't have expected and didn't want. As my last evening fell, I was returning from the Guaza cliffs that I'd visited on my first day. Above a cove a man and woman unloaded three boxes from a car and to my sixth sense their contents were no mystery.

The breathing holes were one clue. I lurked and watched as the hapless birds they contained would be pulled out and released back to sea. From rocks five metres above the waves the man held one shearwater up and let it go.

Success. The bird swooped to the water's surface, spread its wings and skimmed away.

The second was a different story.

It didn't seem ready and instead its swoop took it skidding across rocks on the far side of the cove, where it flapped uselessly. The rehabilitator had a third individual in his hands already but weighed his options with that one. While number two floundered on dry land, his companion was returned to the box.

True to instinct, the beached bird tried to scoot itself towards water. He would be hard to recapture if he made it and he did. Now he could swim, but kept attempting to take off. To no avail.

This was becoming heartbreaking. The rescue man – and let's be clear: he was honourably trying to rescue these birds – made his way round to the water's edge but then was at a loss. I guess he was. I could see no way of retrieving the shearwater without a boat, or a long net, and neither appeared to be forthcoming.

I left. I felt so useless. Unable to help a creature already distressed by human agency. It was a sombre coda to the holiday.

Madrid, 2004

I wasn't expecting to score eight lifers in a major European capital but Madrid, as February turned into March, was a surprise, especially as I was focussing on museums.

On the Friday of my arrival that was all I did and saw the usual city birds. But the day after, I found one spotless starling outside the Prado and later I took time out to walk round the Retiro, which is the main green space in the centre of the city. It was cold, so I wasn't hanging around. Fortunately my first problem bird obliged by feeding on the ground close to me and I was able to study it for a while. It was a serin but I needed to note its details because I wasn't carrying a field guide. That necessitates an accurate description of the bird. We shall see how this discipline failed later on.

The next birds should have been easy to identify immediately but they were so unexpected that it took me a while. They'd been calling with high whistles long before I located them. More time elapsed before a good view of one – large bill, white wing bar, pinkish wash on the cheeks and black wing tips. I was thinking along the lines of an exotic finch when it dawned on me that this was my third ever view of hawfinches. And so close this time. They were all around and low down in the bushes – brilliant.

Gulls so far inland weren't an expectation either but I shouldn't have been surprised. One flying over Estanque, the lake in the middle of the park, looked like a yellow-legged but might have been dark enough to be lesser black-backed. There must be some overlap between the two.

On Sunday, the 29th, I walked out into Casa de Campo, where a few tree sparrows mingled with the numerous house sparrows. I didn't see one Spanish sparrow and eventually stopped checking through the plentiful small flocks for them.

It was a long walk in before an eventual distant glimpse of a large white bird with dark markings. I had it down for a white stork straight away despite my field guide noting the species as a summer visitor. This wasn't one of my dodgy identifications because the storks soon became numerous and obvious.

Not long after was another summer visitor – a black kite. I had this as a lifer but entering my sightings days later back in Blighty told me otherwise. I'd logged black kite the year before in Australia and so now assumed that record to be wrong but there were no other candidates for the right bird down under. A quick check on the Web and – lo and behold! – my record was accurate and the kites were the same species – a widespread bird.

During that last day of February I recorded a green woodpecker. I didn't remark on it at the time but it did become remarkable when version 3.5 of the IOU world list split Iberian green woodpecker into its own species, *Picus sharpei*. So, in 2004 I wouldn't have noticed its lack of face mask nor its thinner black border round the malar stripe. Had it been male. The female is more subtly different. Notice that the next time you see our nominate green woodpecker.

So to 1st March and a walk along the Manzanares from El Pardo. This trip delivered in spades with gryphon vultures right away and later, much rarer black vultures. I also came a cropper with cirl buntings. Mine weren't yellow, so I misidentified them as rock buntings even though they had a massive bib. My field guide insisted they didn't, which I ignored. A better book later on forced me to correct my mistake despite not then having my little sketch of them for final confirmation – the pitfall of using a guide in the field!

The day's biggest thrill was a black redstart hawking from a fence. I'd sought this species in Britain without success. Fortunately it is distinctive once you see the colour of the tail.

It was a surprise to see house martins and at first I doubted my glimpse of them. But there were plenty later on and one sand martin. Spring migration was underway. My first Cetti's warblers of the year were also calling the length of the river.

On the Tuesday of my departure I dumped my bags at the airport and went back one stop on the Metro to Parque Juan Carlos I. Being a filler while waiting for my flight, I wasn't expecting much. However, the best bird of the trip bounded past me like a woodpecker – hoopoe! It wasn't a lifer but one can't grow sick of them.

A Sardinian warbler was a nice find and my stroll did round off with one life species – a couple of crested larks. So, I can recommend Madrid for a combination of culture and birding, a rare mix.

Glossary

BirdLife International – a global alliance of conservation organisations working together for the world's birds.

Class – such as *Aves*, birds. Other similar classes are mammals, reptiles, amphibians and so on to make up the vertebrates. See Order.

Endemic – occurring only in a restricted geographic location, which can be as big as a country. Obviously a tad artificial in that case.

Family – a subdivision of an Order of organisms. A family such as the chats and flycatchers, aka Muscicapidae, contains species, like stonechat and robin, grouped by Genus. See also Order.

Genus – a group of Species with some sufficiently big difference from another Genus, such as *Erithacus* in the Muscicapidae family. Its name forms the first word of the Scientific Name, e.g. *Erithacus rubecula* for robin. See Family.

IBA – Important Bird Area as identified by BirdLife International.

IOU – International Ornithologists' Union, source of the taxonomy used throughout this book, despite what any other field guide may say; to confuse matters this taxonomy is called the IOC World Bird List. See their website to unravel that nomenclature!

LBJ – little brown job, always a passerine that skulks.

Life List – an enumeration of all the species of bird seen throughout the world, and so...

Lifer – a new species for the Life List.

Lores – facial feathers between the eye and the bill.

Mega – a bird that's beyond rare for a given location.

Order – a subdivision of a Class of organisms, such as *Charadriiformes*, shorebirds. See also Family.

Passerine - the bird Order, Passeriformes, that constitutes more than half the species in the world. Basically they're the littler birds towards the end of most field guides – the birds that perch and sing and visit feeding stations. In other words, not your waterfowl, seabirds, raptors, gamebirds, pigeons, woodpeckers and so on, though the latter two do come to feeders.

Scientific Name – under the system devised by Linnaeus the label for a Species, such as *Podiceps cristatus*, the first word being the name of its Genus. Always italicised, it's the *lingua franca* for taxonomists around the world in preference to localised common names.

Tick – an addition to a list, such as Life List, Patch List, county list.

Twitch – a flocking of birdwatchers to a rare or mega bird.